WITNESS TO WAR

THE VIETNAM WAR

KELLY ROBERTS

What can we learn from the people who witnessed war?

CHERITON
CHILDREN'S BOOKS

Published in 2025 by **Cheriton Children's Books**
1 Bank Drive West, Shrewsbury, Shropshire, SY3 9DJ, UK

Copyright 2025 Cheriton Children's Books

First Edition

Author: Kelly Roberts
Designer: Paul Myerscough
Editor: Sarah Eason
Proofreader: Katie Dicker

Picture credits: Cover: Australian War Memorial/Michael Coleridge; Inside: p1: National Archives and Records Administration, p3: Alamy/NARA, p4: United States Armed Forces, p5: National Archives and Records Administration, p6: Shutterstock/Jorisvo, p7: National Archives and Records Administration, p8: National Archives and Records Administration, p9: Australian War Memorial/Michael Coleridge, p10: Wikimedia Commons, p11: National Archives and Records Administration, p12: U.S. Information Agency, p13: National Archives, p14: United States Army, p15: National Archives, p16: National Archives and Records Administration, p19b: National Archives and Records Administration, p19t: Library of Congress, p20: US Army/SP4 Dennis J. Kurpius, 221st Signal Company (Pic), p21: Department of Defense (USMC), p22: Library of Congress/Ronald L. Haeberle, p22t: Library of Congress/Ronald L. Haeberle, p23: Shutterstock/Marco Gallo, p24: Alamy/Eye Ubiquitous, p25b: US military, p25t: Associated Press/Nick Ut, p27: Lyndon B. Johnson Library/Frank Wolfe, p28: Department of Defense, p29: National Archives and Records Administration/Sergeant William F. Dickman, p30b: National Archives and Records Administration, p30t: National Archives and Records Administration/PFC David Epstein, p31: National Archives, p32: Shutterstock/Bill Ragan, p33: United States Army Institute of Heraldry/Meyerson, Joel D, p34: US Navy/PH2 Phil Eggman, p35: National Archives and Records Administration, p36: Shutterstock/Thanachet Maviang, p37: Shutterstock/Steph Photographies, p38: United States Armed Forces, p39: Alamy/CPA Media Pte Ltd, p40: National Archives and Records Administration, p41: Shutterstock/De Jongh Photography, p42: Shutterstock/Lissandra Melo, p43: Alamy/NARA.

Printed in China

Please visit our website,
www.cheritonchildrensbooks.com
to see more of our high-quality books.

CONTENTS

CHAPTER 1

THE VIETNAM WAR

The Vietnam War lasted just over 20 years. The fighting and bombing killed and injured millions of people from several different countries, and the horrific experience of the long war caused millions more to suffer from long-term mental disorders. For every one of those millions, there was a family who grieved for the death of a loved one or who had to come to terms with the effect of the war on their lives. All witnessed the devastation of war—and in doing so, became a witness to history. In this book we will look at some of their stories and their words as witnesses to war.

For some children in Vietnam, life was full of hardship. Fighting, explosions, gunfire, and fear dominated their world.

WITNESSES TO WAR

In this book we will hear the words of witnesses to the war: the people who experienced the conflict firsthand. We'll discover what impact the war had on them and what we can learn from their accounts. In each case, read the source and the notes, then try to answer the questions.

A War of Words

The Vietnam War pitted the United States against the **communist** North Vietnamese in a fight over South Vietnam. The Americans named the conflict the "Vietnam War." The North Vietnamese and their supporters named it the "American War," or, in full, the "War Against the Americans to Save the Nation."

North and South

The North Vietnamese wanted to free South Vietnam from the influence of western countries and to bring it under communist control. The South Vietnamese government wanted to remain independent and were **allies** of the United States and other western countries. The United States did not want South Vietnam to be taken over by communists. **Civilians** in South Vietnam were divided over what they wanted for their country.

Understanding PRIMARY SOURCES

The eyewitness accounts in this book are primary sources. A primary source provides direct information about a subject. Examples of primary sources include diaries and letters. Along with the eyewitness accounts in the book, we will also look at some other primary sources, such as photos and drawings, which provide important information about war and the experience of war.

For people in the United States and other countries that sent troops to Vietnam, the war meant missing a parent, child, or other loved one, and living with the often-terrible consequences of a ruthless conflict.

Vietnam and the United States

The build-up to the Vietnam War was complicated and steeped in **colonial** control. France, a colonial power, had ruled Vietnam since the nineteenth century. The start of World War II (1939–1945) presented a Vietnamese communist named Ho Chi Minh—meaning "He Who Enlightens"—with the chance to prepare his country for independence from France. He called his organization the Vietminh, which means the League for the Independence of Vietnam.

Vietnam Under Foreign Rule

In 1941, the Japanese took control of the countries under France's colonial rule, including Vietnam. The Vietminh fought against the Japanese and managed to take control of parts of North Vietnam. After the Japanese surrendered in 1945, Ho Chi Minh declared the country the Democratic Republic of Vietnam. However, the French returned in 1946, and there then followed a period of war in which the French army lost thousands of men in battle. France finally withdrew in 1954.

A Problem to Fix

World powers, including the United States and the Soviet Union, came together in 1954 at an international gathering, called the Geneva Conference, to try to solve the conflict. It was agreed that communist Ho Chi Minh would control the North and an anti-communist named Ngo Dinh Diem would control the South. There would be elections, and Vietnamese people could decide in which part of the country they wished to live. However, Ngo Dinh Diem refused to hold elections.

Ho Chi Minh established the Vietminh in 1941.

A Fear of Communism

The United States dreaded the spread of communism, which had already divided another Asian country, Korea, into South and North. Former President Dwight Eisenhower, shown here in 1957, and his advisors met with the South Vietnam President Ngo Dinh Diem to discuss their concerns and encourage a more democratic government in South Vietnam to try and prevent the further spread of communism.

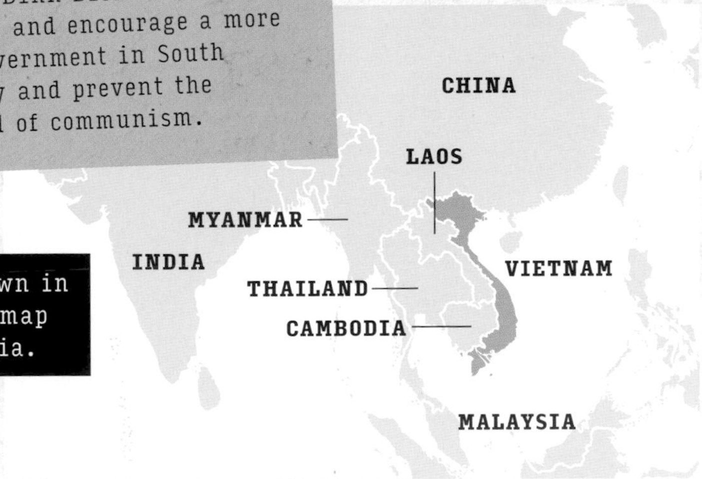

CHINA

LAOS

MYANMAR —

INDIA

THAILAND —

CAMBODIA —

VIETNAM

MALAYSIA

Vietnam is shown in purple on this map of Southeast Asia.

Popular with the People

In the North, the Vietminh had established strong control with the support of the **peasant** community. It had achieved this partly by giving back land to the peasants from wealthier landowners. Meanwhile, in the South, Diem's rule was **corrupt** and unpopular, and he was imprisoning his **opponents**. The Vietminh began to support those groups resisting Diem in the South.

These groups went on to form the National Liberation Front (NLF) which was more commonly called the Vietcong by the Americans.

Going to War

Tensions and fighting increased between the North and South Vietnamese, with the United States sending more aid and military support to the South. In 1965, the United States acknowledged it was at war.

CHAPTER 2

A COMPLEX WAR

The Vietnam War killed and injured millions of soldiers and civilians. Men and women on both sides of the conflict were directly caught up in the **atrocities**. Across the world, families felt the devastating impact of the war.

The Heartache of War

American soldiers had not long returned from fighting in the Korean War, which ended in 1953. In one generation, a father who had fought in Korea might have then fought in Vietnam, and his son might also be called up to fight in Vietnam. The Vietnamese had also been involved in fighting France and Japan before the Vietnam War began. All countries involved in the Vietnam War had already experienced the agonizing heartache and loss caused by fighting in a long conflict.

PRIMARY SOURCE

Dealing with the Draft

As the involvement of the United States in the war increased, men over the age of 18 were called up and had to serve in the army. This was known as the draft. Until 1969, people who went to college avoided the draft, but generally this was only affordable for families who were wealthy enough to pay for their child's education. This meant that many young men from poorer families, including many Black men like this soldier, were sent to Vietnam. What effect do you think that may have had on those families and their communities?

WITNESS TO WAR

This is the account of Alan Jones of the Royal Australian Air Force (RAAF). He served in the war, and remembers here his first experience of the conflict.

What do you think Alan means by "he tried hard not to concentrate on the noise"? What noise may he have been referring to?

"My first impression of being in combat? I have never been so scared in my life. No question about it. I couldn't swallow, I remember it was very hard to swallow ... I knew what I had to do, but it was getting my mind to function ... I tried not to concentrate on the noise and do my job. Sometimes, it was pretty hard. I take my hat off to the ground forces because you would not have got me walking around down there amongst all that."

What does this section of Alan's account tell us about what it may have been like to be a member of the ground forces during the war?

Boots on the Ground

The battlefield for the Vietnam War stretched right across Vietnam. Hundreds of thousands of troops from various countries scoured the land, engaging the enemy. Untrained fighters formed a key part of the North Vietnamese force.

The Tide Turns

When Ngo Dinh Diem refused to honor the agreement of 1954 to hold elections, many South Vietnamese turned against him. As Diem **persecuted** those who disagreed with him, many of his opponents fled to the rain forest, where Ho Chi Minh helped organize them into the NLF (or Vietcong) and supplied them with weapons.

Soldiers from the South

South Vietnam's army, the Army of the Republic of Vietnam (ARVN), was made up of poorly trained young men, who were forced to serve in the army for two years. This was hard for their families, who relied on them to work the land. Many ARVN soldiers took family members to live with them in their camps. This meant they stayed together as families, but the living conditions in camps were poor.

Soldiers from the North

The North Vietnamese army (NVA) was an efficient army. Young men were drafted in to fight and to help organize the support systems that enabled the army to travel with equipment and weapons to the south. They traveled on a network of mountain and rain forest paths called the Ho Chi Minh Trail.

The Ho Chi Minh Trail was used to carry vital supplies south to waiting troops.

WITNESS TO WAR

This is the account of Ngoc Minh Ngo, whose
father was a soldier in the South Vietnamese army.
Her father's brother fought on the opposite side.

A guerrilla fighter is
a person who does
not fight as part of
an official army.

"My father was a colonel in the South
Vietnamese army ... Like many of his peers,
he left school to join the Vietminh, seeking
independence from French colonial rule. He
became a guerrilla fighter, living and hiding in
remote areas to avoid capture by the French.
When the country was divided in two, he
chose to remain in the south while his younger
brother and many of his friends went north.
For two decades, they fought on opposite sides,
but after the war, my father and his brother
reconnected as soon as they could. The years
of war did nothing to alter their bond."

What do you think it may have been
like for family members and friends to
have been divided by war in this way?

Women Caught up in War

Women fought for both the Vietcong and the North Vietnamese army (NVA). In the United States forces, women did not go into combat but worked in crucial areas, such as nursing and communication, and for aid organizations, including the International Red Cross. Women often endured the same harsh conditions as the soldiers. Many female journalists traveled to Vietnam to report on a war that divided American opinion.

An Army of Nurses

Ninety percent of the women in the US army in Vietnam worked as nurses. The use of helicopters in the war enabled a quick transfer for injured soldiers to makeshift hospitals, where nurses had much greater responsibility for decision-making and treatment than in previous conflicts. These women saw and treated terrible injuries.

Single-Parent Families

When the men were fighting in Vietnam, mothers at home were left to bring up and care for their children. For American soldiers, a **tour of duty** was nearly one year long. The women left behind had to cope with the absence of their partner and suffer anxiety about their safety.

Vietnamese women on both sides of the war were called into combat as well as caring for families and their homes. This young woman is patrolling an area around her village to try and protect it from the Vietcong.

Key Players

Women played vital roles during the war. They were active in the community, providing health care for Vietnamese families, as well as wounded soldiers. This became even more important as the war continued and families suffered from a lack of food.

Hard Labor

In North Vietnam, men were drafted to fight for the NVA. This meant that women had all the responsibility and work of farming their land, as well as bringing up their children. Women were also expected to help protect villages in the North from American **bombardment**.

WITNESS TO WAR

Nurses who traveled to Vietnam to assist during the war offered medical support to soldiers, but also to local people. They often had to deal with extreme danger and trauma. This is the account of one US army nurse, Diane Evans:

"We were in a very dangerous place in Vietnam ... I remember the sound of shrapnel and the sound of thuds and rockets and mortars and that horrible, terrifying sound. But we didn't have time to be afraid. What we did was run to our patients ...."

Shrapnel is pieces of sharp metal from exploding bombs.

What impact do you think being in such personal danger but having to tend to the needs of their patients may have had on nurses during the war?

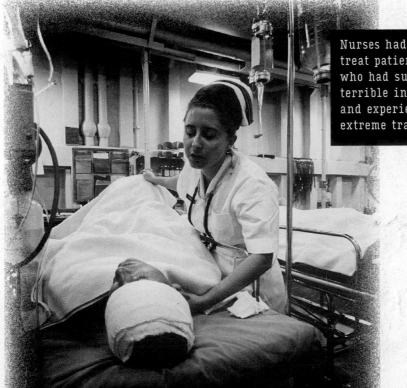

Nurses had to treat patients who had suffered terrible injuries and experienced extreme trauma.

CHAPTER 3

A DIFFICULT FIGHT

United States troops found it difficult to cope with the thick, hot, and humid rain forest conditions. Also, despite their relentless bombing campaigns and sophisticated weapons, they were unprepared for their enemy's methods. The tactics on both sides were devastating for all the families, whatever side they supported.

Advantages and Ambushes

The eventual success of the NVA and Vietcong was due largely to their guerrilla tactics. The Vietcong improvised many of their weapons from whatever they could find. They used US bombs that had not exploded and created **lethal booby traps**, such as deadly sharp spikes hidden in the ground. The Vietcong had the advantage of knowing the land and being used to the conditions. They **ambushed** enemy soldiers and stayed so close to them that US forces were unable to attack them from the air without risking the lives of their own men.

Deadly Disguises

The Vietcong disguised themselves as peasants, the very people US troops were trying to protect. The Americans, therefore, began to suspect everyone, often with horrific consequences for innocent civilians and their homes.

These villagers were captured by the United States army, suspected of being members of the Vietcong.

Road of Weapons

The Soviet Union and China supplied the NVA with weapons and rockets, which were then transported to the Vietcong along the Ho Chi Minh Trail. This rain forest route wound through the neighboring countries of Laos and Cambodia. The Americans were at first reluctant to attack the Ho Chi Minh Trail because it could draw Laos and Cambodia into the conflict, further stretching US troops.

Terrifying Tunnels

The Vietcong built a complex underground network of tunnels through which they moved from place to place, hidden from view. These tunnels were home to hospitals, training grounds, and army headquarters. When a network of tunnels was discovered, the US, Australian, or New Zealand army sent down one soldier, known as a tunnel rat, to try and blow it up. Entering tunnels was extremely dangerous, because the Vietcong laid booby traps in the tunnels.

PRIMARY SOURCE

Adding to the Hardship

These US soldiers are carrying a fellow wounded soldier on a stretcher through thick rain forest swamp. These conditions were new to many soldiers and added to the difficulties of their experience. What do you think it must have been like to try to navigate the rain forest terrain and how might that have affected the **morale** of US soldiers?

Daily Dangers

For Americans, the Vietnam War, like World War I (1914–1918) and World War II (1939–1945), was fought on foreign soil. Families suffered loss and anxiety about their loved ones, but day-to-day life in the United States, Australia, New Zealand, or South Korea was not under threat. However, in Vietnam, daily life was terrifying for everyone.

Relentless Risks

Innocent people could walk over a Vietcong mine or be caught up in a US bombing raid and be killed or disabled for life. Simple tasks such as getting water from a well became terrifying and dangerous. Civilians running from bombs or gunfire were often shot.

PRIMARY SOURCE

Caught in the Crossfire

This Vietnamese mother and her child are hiding from gunfire with US soldiers. Mothers and children faced horror during the war. They risked being targeted by the Vietcong for supporting the United States and its allies, they risked being killed in **crossfire**, and they risked being attacked by US soldiers if they were thought to be communist sympathizers. What long-term effect do you think such terror would have had on women and children?

WITNESS TO WAR

This is the account of Nguyen Van Phuoc, who was a Vietnamese child during the war. His mother was killed by the US army when they attacked his village.

What effect do you think such devastating attacks by the US army may have had on the Vietnamese people? How may it have affected their view of the United States?

" An American force ... set fire to all our houses. They were clearing the area of civilians so we couldn't provide support for [guerillas]. We moved to another village but ... returned home. On that night when the soldiers moved into the village ... they shot my mother in the head, killing her. Her name was Lan. The American soldiers killed 13 people that night, all women, children, and old people. ... I was 9 years old. I ran with my brother on my back. My brother and I went to stay with our grandmother."

Moving Out

Diem, the South Vietnamese president, had put in place a very unpopular policy of forcing peasants to move to **fortified** villages, away from communist influence. The US army also created special areas where villagers were forced to move. These moves succeeded only in creating more support for the communists.

Death and Destruction

When US soldiers arrived in areas suspected of supporting the NVA or Vietcong, they often destroyed homes and villages. This encouraged more support for the Vietcong. Many families who had lived peacefully with other villagers now found themselves supporting the North Vietnamese, an **alliance** that put them in danger from the occupying troops.

Impossible Choices

Peasants in villages in South Vietnam faced terrible choices. If they supported the Vietcong or communists, and offered them shelter or food, they risked attack from the Americans. If they supported the Americans, they risked punishment from the Vietcong.

CHAPTER 4

A FIGHT FAR AWAY

Troops from the United States, Australia, New Zealand, and South Korea were fighting a war miles from their homeland. United States troops were sent on tours of duty that lasted nearly a year. During that time, families at home witnessed some of the horrors of war on television and in newspapers. For every soldier or nurse fighting or working in Vietnam, there was a mother, father, sister, brother, wife, husband, or partner worrying about a loved one.

Lost Letters

Communication between the soldiers in Vietnam and families at home was mainly by letter, although some men were occasionally able to get to a telephone. Some letters were never sent, since the soldier was killed or captured before being able to mail it.

WITNESS TO WAR

Letters from one soldier, Sergeant Steve Flaherty, came to light more than 40 years after they were written. A Vietcong soldier had taken them from the young man's body after he had died.

"I felt bullets going past me," he wrote. "I have never been so scared in my life." In another letter, he wrote, "The NVA soldiers fought until they died and one even booby trapped himself, and when we approached him, he blew himself up and took two of our men with him."

What do Steve's words tell us about the experience of soldiers fighting the war, far from home, and against an enemy that was prepared to kill itself in order to kill US soldiers?

Missing in Action

Families dreaded a knock at the door informing them that a family member had been killed. Some families still do not know what happened to their loved ones. These soldiers were described as "missing in action (MIA)". There are 1,642 US soldiers that remain unaccounted for. The fate of many Vietnamese soldiers is also still unknown.

When the grim reality of the Vietnam War became apparent on televisions and in newspapers, people began to question it.

PRIMARY SOURCE

Losses on All Sides

Many US and Vietnamese soldiers disappeared during the war; their bodies were never found but they are believed dead. This woman did discover the fate of her husband— he was killed. She is shown here mourning him, his wrapped body laid on the ground before her. What do you think these images of suffering tell us about the human impact of war, and what can we learn from them?

The Horror of War

The Vietnam War shocked the world with the brutality committed by soldiers on both sides and the extent to which innocent civilians were caught up in the fight. Those who survived the war were often wounded, physically or emotionally.

Many soldiers carried out terrible and cruel acts. Soldiers returned home, often confused and damaged by their experience. Some became addicted to drugs that had been readily available while on tour of duty. The horror of the war would change their lives, as well as those of their families.

PRIMARY SOURCE

Witnessing Brutality

This photograph shows young soldiers during a moment of **respite** from the fighting. They were sent to Vietnam unprepared for what was to come. They saw fellow soldiers and friends suffer excruciating injury and death. They faced an enemy who evaded them with skill and savagery. They were part of a war that many people did not want to fight. How do you think that may have affected their psychology during the fighting?

Bruce Palmer, who was a US army general during the Vietnam War, wrote of his experience decades later. These are his words:

What do you think Bruce means by "having to react and dance to the enemy's tune"?

"The enemy clearly had the initiative. Given the way the United States had decided to fight the war in a passive defense of South Vietnam, American forces found themselves in the unenviable situation of having to react and dance to the enemy's tune."

Many soldiers were taken as prisoners of war by the NVA and were often tortured and badly treated while in captivity.

Capture and Campaigns

In 1965, Commander James B. Stockdale was leading an air raid over a North Vietnamese oil refinery when his A-4E Skyhawk plane was shot down. Stockdale landed in a rice field, where he was taken prisoner by the North Vietnamese army. He remained a prisoner of war (POW) for more than seven years, enduring beatings and torture. Back home, his wife Sybil campaigned for families of POWs to be given more information and support from the government and army about their captured relatives.

Shocking Sights

During the course of the Vietnam War there were some terrible atrocities that ripped apart the lives of families. Americans were deeply shocked to see images and hear reports of their soldiers behaving in inhumane and callous ways.

An Act of Horror

On March 16, 1968, US troops entered a South Vietnamese village called My Lai. They gathered about 400 women, children, and elderly men, lined them up, and shot them. Perhaps the soldiers may have believed that the villagers had been helping the enemy, but there is no evidence of this. The soldiers killed innocent people. They took out their frustration, anger, and confusion at the lack of progress and success in the war on innocent civilians. They were angry that their Vietnamese enemy was often hidden but still deadly.

US soldiers set fire to homes during the My Lai massacre.

A Cover-Up

The army hushed up the **massacre**, but a year after the terrible event, it was uncovered by a journalist. The discovery of the shocking events fueled the anti-war movement and horrified those Americans and allies who had supported the war. Lieutenant William Calley, who had led the attack, returned to the United States to face murder charges. He was sentenced to life imprisonment but was released within four years.

Families like this one were killed during the My Lai tragedy. It was a shocking event that changed many people's view of the war when the story was later revealed.

WITNESS TO WAR

These are the words of two US soldiers who witnessed the My Lai massacre:

Larry La Croix, US army sergeant—

"It was terrible. They were slaughtering villagers like so many sheep."

What do the words "slaughtering villagers like so many sheep" tell us about the scale of the horrors carried out during the event?

Leonard Gonzales, US army soldier—

"That day it was just a massacre. Just plain right out, wiping out people."

This relief mural in the Martyrs Cemetery in Hoi An, Vietnam, shows a battle of the war. Ordinary men and women as well as soldiers can be seen in the relief, showing the scale of the war and its effect on the civilians of Vietnam.

The Young Suffer

One of the most devastating and infamous images from the Vietnam War is of a terrified girl, naked, with her skin burned, running toward a photographer. This is the story of an innocent young girl whose life was turned upside down by the effects of the war in her country.

Children in a Crisis

In 1972, nine-year-old Phan Thi Kim Phúc was living with her family in a South Vietnamese village, Trang Bàng, over which the North and South Vietnamese were fighting for control. Kim Phúc was with her friends and family when a South Vietnamese airplane mistakenly started bombing a **Buddhist** pagoda in the village. The bombs were packed with napalm (see below).

Surviving but Scarred

When the bombs fell, Kim Phúc, her friends, and her relatives ran. Two of Kim Phúc's young brothers were killed instantly. The napalm burned through Kim Phúc's skin. A Vietnamese photographer took the picture opposite before whisking Kim Phúc to the hospital. He remained in contact with her as she underwent numerous operations to heal the terrible burns that had eaten through to her bones. Kim Phúc was one of many thousands of children terribly wounded or killed in the war.

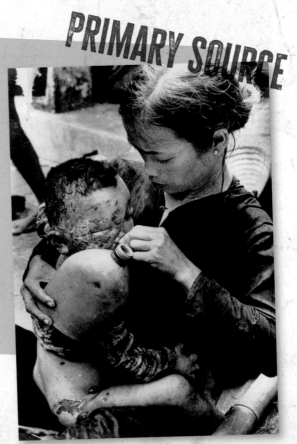

Napalm Nightmare

This child was horribly injured by napalm, which is a mixture of gasoline and a chemical. Napalm creates a thick gel that sticks to the skin. When the gel is on fire, it burns for a long time, often burning victims through to the muscle and bone, causing excruciating pain. Why do you think the US army and its allies were prepared to use such a devastating weapon during the war?

PRIMARY SOURCE

Kim Phúc survived
the terrifying
attack by tearing off
her burning clothes.

Surprise Attacks

In 1968, the Vietcong agreed to a
ceasefire for the celebration of Tet,
the Vietnamese New Year. However,
as innocent families were preparing
to celebrate, the Vietcong traveled to
cities in South Vietnam, pretending
to see relatives. They surprised the
US forces with attacks on Saigon and
other cities. Thousands were killed.

Starved and Desperate

Not only did the US army
use chemicals to attack the
Vietnamese, but it also used
them to destroy the country's
economy. Vietnam depended
mainly on farming income. The
US army sprayed a **herbicide**
called "Agent Blue" onto crops to
deprive the North Vietnamese
of their food supply. Between
1962 and 1969, 688,000 acres
(278,400 ha) of agricultural land
was sprayed—mainly fields of
crops. During and after the war,
food was scarce and families
struggled to feed themselves.
Twenty years of war had
shattered Vietnam's economy.

South Vietnamese
soldiers defend
Saigon during the
Tet Offensive.

CHAPTER 5

LOSING FAITH

Until 1965, the United States' involvement in Vietnam was not clear-cut, although forces were active in the South. However, increased attacks on American troops pushed the United States into committing itself to a war to stop the spread of communism into South Vietnam.

Different Views

As the war continued with publicized disasters, such as the Tet Offensive, and little progress in stopping the North Vietnamese, many people both at home and in combat became increasingly **disillusioned**. The war exposed huge divisions in United States society. Some families were proud of their loved ones' bravery in fighting for their country; others were ashamed of the behavior of their soldiers.

Shock and Anger

The Vietnam War was played out in front of war reporters, photographers, and television cameras. The work of journalists and war photographers gave detailed descriptions of the horror of the war. The media spotlight threw a different light on the war. People around the world watched television images of young men dying and suffering catastrophic injuries. They saw shocking images of their soldiers treating other humans badly. Public opinion in the United States, Australia, and New Zealand was divided and led to angry demonstrations.

Against the War

On May 4, 1970, the US National Guard fired into a group of anti-war demonstrators at Kent State University in Ohio. Four students were killed. This sparked further anti-war demonstrations and riots on hundreds of other campuses.

A Cruel Protest

In New Zealand, some service families received terrible phone calls telling them that their loved one had been killed in the war. However, this turned out to be a cruel hoax by a group of anti-war protesters.

WITNESS TO WAR

Jeannette Rankin, former US congresswoman and anti-war campaigner, spoke out against the war in 1968. These are her words:

Why do you think Jeannette calls upon American women to end the war?

"It is unconscionable that 10,000 boys have died in Vietnam. If 10,000 American women had mind enough, they could end the war, if they were committed to the task—even if it meant going to jail."

Why do you think Jeanette thought that women may have been more inclined than men to end the war?

Increasing numbers of people took part in anti-war campaigns when the true horror of the Vietnam war came to light.

GET THE HELL OUT OF VIETNAM

Heroes and Hatred

Often, men returning home from war are called war heroes. This was not always the case for those returning from Vietnam. They often faced **hostility**, anger, and abuse. Some were spat at and even advised not to wear their uniforms in public.

Dealing with the Horror

Many of the United States soldiers were disillusioned about the war while they were in Vietnam. To cope with the horror of their experience, some turned to drugs that were easily available. These soldiers returned to the United States, often with a serious addiction to drugs. As the withdrawal of forces began, the mood among the troops dropped even more, as they knew they risked being killed in a war they were not going to win.

A Slow Exit

Peace talks began in 1968 but they never amounted to more than talk. When Richard Nixon became US president in 1969, he committed to withdrawing American troops from Vietnam. To support this, he announced the policy called "Vietnamization"—training and equipping the South Vietnamese army to enable the United States to reduce troop numbers.

A War That Can't Be Won

Hue was one of the South Vietnamese cities attacked during the war. Almost 5,000 government officials and civilians who had worked with the Americans were executed, and 100,000 civilians became **refugees** as their city was destroyed. The Americans eventually regained control of the cities of South Vietnam, but the American public began to realize they might not win this war.

The Cost of War

During the mid-1960s, there were serious riots in the United States, with people protesting at poor housing and lack of money for schools and hospitals. Many people linked these issues to the vast amounts of money soaked up to fund the war.

During the three years following Richard Nixon's election, more than 500,000 soldiers were withdrawn from Vietnam.

After years of war and suffering terrible injuries and trauma, many US soldiers were demoralized by the war and wanted an end to it.

WITNESS TO WAR

Harry Summers was a US colonel during the war. He later became a historian. This is his account:

"By 1968, the public had given us four years, their money, and their sons. So, I don't blame the American people. I do blame the national leadership, including the military leadership, for not setting clear and definable goals and objectives."

What do you think Harry means by "not setting clear and definable goals and objectives"?

Lasting Wounds

Many Vietnam War soldiers returned to their home country and resumed strong relationships with their families, found employment, and were as content as anyone else. However, others faced continued difficulties because of their experiences during the war. This in turn had a huge effect on their families.

After the Trauma

Many men suffered from **post-traumatic stress disorder (PTSD)** after the Vietnam War, with nightmares, flashbacks, and mental health issues. During their tour in Vietnam they had witnessed terrible deaths, the wounding of comrades, and killing all around them, while living with the fear of an unseen enemy. Often, the PTSD was so severe that the returning soldiers were unable to find work, hold down a job, or maintain close relationships.

Soldiers had carried out and witnessed countless horrors during the Vietnam War.

The brutal scenes they had witnessed during the war caused many soldiers to experience PTSD afterward.

Many US soldiers would never recover from what they had experienced.

Damaged Families

Families longed for the return of their loved ones. Their expectation was to resume family life as it had been before the war. However, men and women suffering from PTSD were often withdrawn, moody, and unpredictable. This had a damaging effect on their partners, parents, and children.

Healing the Nation

In 1974, US President Gerald Ford offered "draft dodgers" and **deserters** an **amnesty**— they would not be prosecuted for deliberately avoiding service in the armed forces. Ford stated that "**reconciliation** calls for an act of mercy to bind the nation's wounds and to heal the scars of divisiveness."

WITNESS TO WAR

Some men were given a "dishonorable discharge" when they left the army. This meant they left with a bad record, or "paper," perhaps for bad behavior. These are the words of one soldier who was discharged dishonorably:

"But after I came home from Vietnam, I couldn't even get my job back as a dishwasher because of my bad paper ... My discharge status has been a lifetime scar."

What do the soldier's words tell us about the effect of the discharge on **veterans**' lives?

CHAPTER 6

A LASTING HORROR

As the United States began to realize it could not win the war, it started to withdraw from South Vietnam. In 1973, the last troops left—the American men were coming home. However, in Vietnam the fighting was far from over. For Vietnamese families, the horror of the war continued long after the troops pulled out.

Victory to the North

Within nine months, a ceasefire that had been agreed earlier was quickly broken. Without the strength of the US army behind it, the South Vietnamese army struggled. Its leaders were often corrupt and ineffective. The North Vietnamese advanced on the south with relentless force. In 1975, South Vietnam surrendered to North Vietnam. North Vietnamese troops entered Saigon, which was later renamed Ho Chi Minh City.

Children were left **orphans** because of the war, with the responsibility of caring for younger siblings. Many had never known life without war. Building a future after the war would be very difficult for them, and many never overcame the trauma they had experienced.

A Destroyed Country

The Vietnamese were left with bombed cities, like the one shown below, and destroyed farms and villages. The people had been at war with each other for years. For the people who had witnessed the terror that had enveloped the country, they would now face the challenge of rebuilding shattered homes and lives. How do you think they may have felt when faced with this after the horrors of the war?

One Country

The whole of Vietnam was now under the control of North Vietnam's communist government. The northern city of Hanoi was its new capital. On July 2, 1976, North and South of the country became one nation, named the Socialist Republic of Vietnam (SRV). The country was united on paper, but it had suffered over 20 years of war and divisions between the North and the South were still strong. The Vietnamese faced an uncertain future as they picked up the pieces again.

The Suffering Continued

American and other returning troops had to rebuild their lives back in their home countries, but the Vietnamese had to rebuild their country as well as their lives. Hundreds of thousands of South Vietnamese were killed. Millions more were sent to "reeducation camps," which were, in reality, prison camps. There, they had to suffer terrible conditions and physical abuse. Yet more families were torn apart, as their loved ones were killed or died in these camps.

A Country in Chaos

When the North Vietnamese advanced on Saigon, the Americans desperately airlifted any remaining personnel from the city. There were chaotic scenes as many South Vietnamese tried to leave the country.

Boat People

Many people wanted to leave Vietnam. Some wanted to escape the poverty that the war had brought to the country. Others wanted to escape persecution from the winning communists. The refugees became known as "boat people," as they took to the seas to escape and begin new lives. More than 2 million Vietnamese sought to leave their country.

Dangerous Journeys

The desperate refugees often traveled in small, overcrowded fishing boats, hoping to settle in other countries. Many died before reaching dry land. Pirates attacked their boats, stealing and killing. Storms battered the small, flimsy fishing boats, and countless refugees drowned.

PRIMARY SOURCE

Sailing to Safety?

Vietnamese refugees packed into small boats like this one to escape their war-torn country. Men, women, and children braved the waves of the South China Sea in their attempt to find refuge elsewhere. If they survived the journey to another country, what do you think life would have been like for them there? Consider all that they had already experienced during the war and the challenges that may have faced them as they attempted to build a new life.

Trying to Save the Young

When Saigon fell to the communists in April 1975, there were rumors that people associated with the United States might be massacred. President Gerald Ford announced plans to **evacuate** 2,000 orphans. This was named Operation Babylift. Tragically, the first official flight crashed in the rice fields outside Saigon, killing around 140 people, most of them children. However, the evacuation continued for another three weeks.

Changed Forever

Grandparents, uncles, aunts, brothers, sisters, and parents might have been separated in the desperation to leave Vietnam. Once the war was over, families had to come to terms with the way their lives had been devastated.

President Gerald Ford is shown here holding one of the Vietnamese babies transported from Vietnam and taken to the United States.

WITNESS TO WAR

Tom Glenn served during the war and has spoken openly about his experiences. He witnessed the terror that local people felt when Saigon was about to fall.

" ... A Vietnamese army officer I knew planned to escape with his wife and his three children as soon as the US ambassador issued an evacuation order. But when the ambassador chose not to call for an evacuation, the officer, to escape capture, torture, and execution by the victorious North Vietnamese, shot ... his three children, his wife, and himself."

What do Tom's words tell us about how terrified people must have been at the thought of the approaching Vietcong?

Other Conflicts

The Vietnam War ended for American soldiers in 1973. For Vietnamese families, the chaos and fear of war continued for many more years. War also spread to the neighboring countries of Cambodia and Laos. President Nixon had begun to bomb Cambodia in 1969 because its rain forest border had been used as a base for attacks on the South Vietnamese army and its allies, and as a route to transport men and equipment into South Vietnam.

A Devastating Battle

Cambodia had a pro-American government but an opposing communist guerrilla force there, called the Khmer Rouge were allies of North Vietnam. When the South Vietnamese and US troops invaded cambodia in 1970, the Khmer Rouge engaged them in a brutal battle.

Terror in Cambodia

The Khmer Rouge were eventually successful in 1975, and this started a terrible period for Cambodians, and indeed for the Vietnamese. The communist regime was brutal, murdering anyone considered unsympathetic to its views. Up to 2 million people are estimated to have died at the hands of the Khmer Rouge.

Thousands of Cambodians were tortured and killed in this building at the hands of the Khmer Rouge. Photographs of the victims line the walls of what is now a Cambodian museum.

Violence and Horror

Hundreds of thousands of Cambodians fled the country with horrifying tales of violence. The Khmer Rouge led raids on Vietnamese villages along its borders, forcing Vietnamese families to flee their homes. In 1978, Vietnam itself had invaded Cambodia. This war with Cambodia led to the deaths of yet more young Vietnamese.

Brutal Bombings

In 1964, fearing the spread of communism in Laos, which was a **neutral** country, the United States had begun a secret bombing campaign. Over a nine-year period, it dropped 260 million bombs on the country, many of which did not explode. They remained hidden in the ground and exploded unexpectedly. An estimated 20,000 Lao people have been injured or killed by these weapons since the end of the bombing campaign.

Abandoned tanks and unexploded bombs remain in Laos to this day. More than 60 accidents caused by unexploded bombs were recorded in 2021.

WITNESS TO WAR

Robert Sam Anson was a US journalist reporting in Vietnam when he was captured by the Vietcong. This is his account:

"They weren't ... my enemy. I never considered the people of Vietnam or Cambodia or Laos to be my enemy. I believed in peace ... and so they treated me like a friend ... We really got to be brothers."

What do you think we can learn from Robert's words that he "believed in peace ... and so they treated me like a friend"?

Children of the Dust

During the long war, many American troops or men working in civilian roles had met Vietnamese women. As a result of these relationships—some very short and others more serious—children were born. These half-Vietnamese, half-American children became known as "Children of the Dust" or "Amerasians."

Devastated Lives

When the NVA advanced on South Vietnam, and US troops and other personnel had left, the women and their Amerasian children were abandoned. These mothers were often shunned by their own communities for having had relationships outside marriage. They faced hostility for their relationships with the enemy. Some of the women panicked and rejected their babies or children.

Moving to the States

For those abandoned children, life was often a struggle. Their different appearance led to discrimination. In 1982, the US Congress passed the Amerasian Immigration Act, which allowed Vietnamese Amerasians to emigrate to the United States. Some children attempted to find their fathers, while others simply wanted to build new lives.

Fleeing in Fear

Waves of people fled Vietnam. Initially, it was those who wanted to escape the advancing NVA and communist rule. Later, when the new Vietnamese government passed a law that targeted people of Chinese descent, many Vietnamese with Chinese **ancestry** left the country.

After Vietnamese families fled the horrors of the war, they had more trauma to face—the struggle of building a life in another country that often did not want them.

For these Vietnamese refugees boarding a US military ship, hardships and struggles still lay ahead as they attempted to carve out new lives overseas.

Still Not Safe

Refugees who survived the journey to another country faced an uncertain future. Many had to live in overcrowded refugee camps before host countries decided whether to accept them. Governments were not always willing to accept people who came with nothing and needed support. Some were sent back to Vietnam. Those who were allowed to stay often faced hostility from people who lived in the host country.

Some countries struggled to provide the home, education, and health care that all families need. Vietnamese refugees wanted to work to support themselves, and often had to learn a new language. Many took jobs below their skill set. Although they tried to make a new life for themselves, many were homesick and wondered if they should have left at all.

Sick from War

Many years have passed since the Vietnam War. However, the war has affected the health of survivors since. Shortly after returning home some veterans fell sick. Some who wanted to have children found that their wives miscarried or their babies had birth defects. It was suspected that these problems were related to "Agent Blue," "Agent Orange," and the other **toxic** herbicides they were exposed to in Vietnam. Veterans began to file claims for compensation, but the soldiers had to prove that the symptoms of sickness had begun within a year of leaving the army.

Chemical Damage

Vietnam is covered in thick rain forest—the perfect hiding place for the Vietcong. During the war, the United States decided to destroy the rain forest cover. One of the chemicals used was known as "Agent Orange." In 1969 alone, 2,555,810 acres (1,034,300 ha) of forest were destroyed using Agent Orange. The effect of the chemical spread farther than the rain forest. Many Vietnamese children were born with birth defects caused by their parents' exposure to Agent Orange.

A Devastating Agent

An estimated 400,000 people have suffered death or permanent injury from exposure to Agent Orange. About 2 million people have suffered from illnesses caused by exposure and 500,000 babies were born with birth defects because their parents were exposed to the horrific chemical.

Decades after the initial spraying of Agent Orange, the Vietnamese people are still suffering from poisoning by the chemical.

The attempt to flush out and kill Vietcong soldiers hiding in the rain forest with the use of chemicals resulted in terrible health issues, and appalling birth defects. This young musician, whose parent was exposed to the chemicals, was born blind.

WITNESS TO WAR

Bui Thi Tron was a soldier in the NVA. His health was badly affected by Agent Orange. This is his account:

"The jungle we operated in was sprayed often with Agent Orange. The trees lost their leaves and the people from that area told us it was because the water was contaminated by dioxin. Now my health is poor. My stomach is not so good and I have pain in my backside and up and down my legs. It started more than ten years ago."

Dioxin is a chemical compound found in Agent Orange.

Research the use of chemical warfare in recent wars, such as the conflict in Syria. Why do you think such warfare is still being used, despite the clear result of chemical warfare in the Vietnam War?

The Price of War

The Vietnam War killed and injured millions. Countless families were left grieving, and millions of children were orphaned. Much of Vietnam's land was destroyed, either by bombs or toxic herbicides, such as Agent Orange. Soldiers from Australia, New Zealand, South Korea, and Thailand, as well as the United States, were scarred forever by the shocking and traumatic experience of the war.

Was It Worth It?

The United States failed to repel the communists from South Vietnam. As a result, Americans questioned the **morality** of the war and the role played by their country. The confidence and pride of Americans was shaken, because the long and costly war saw them withdraw without success. Whether or not the war succeeded for the nations that took part, only individual families could say if their involvement in it had been worth the physical and emotional pain it caused.

The Death Toll

These are the estimated death tolls for troops involved in the Vietnam War.

North Vietnamese and Vietcong: 1.1 million
South Vietnamese: 200,000–250,000
United States: 58,200
South Korea: more than 4,000
Thailand: 350
Australia: more than 300
New Zealand: 37

Two million Vietnamese civilians were killed.

Soldiers who fought during the war are remembered in the Vietnam Veterans Memorial in Washington, D. C.

For many soldiers who did survive the Vietnam War, the terrible conflict would never be fully over. They suffered the long-lasting effects of PTSD and life-changing injuries, which changed the course of their lives.

WITNESS TO WAR

An American soldier, Jonas Freeman, served one tour of duty in Vietnam. He experienced the turning tide of opinion about the war in the United States, and the following hostility to many US soldiers who had fought in Vietnam.

"And so it made me feel bad that I had placed my life on the line for a country that really didn't care anything about me basically, because they were against the war."

What lessons can we learn from Jonas's words about war and its affect on soldiers? What do you think he meant by "a country that really didn't care anything about me."

Millions in Mourning

Beyond the politics, the Vietnam War was a long and appalling period for families throughout Vietnam, the United States, and its allied countries. The shocking death toll left millions of families mourning a loved one or coping with the traumatic emotional and physical problems faced by others.

A TIMELINE FOR WAR

This timeline charts the key events of the long conflict. There is no agreed fixed date for the start of the Vietnam War because the involvement of the United States began long before it intensified its actions in 1965.

1954 | **July 21:** The Geneva Conference agrees the withdrawal of French and Vietminh to either side of boundary lines in Vietnam.

1955 | **February:** President Eisenhower sends civilian and military advisors to train and support the South Vietnamese army.

1960 | **December 20:** The NLF is formed, known to Americans as the Vietcong.

1961 | **May:** President John F. Kennedy sends 400 Special Forces troops to train and advise Ngo Dinh Diem's army in South Vietnam.

1962 | **Summer:** Australia sends advisors, and later troops, to support South Vietnam. New Zealand does the same the following April.

1963 | **June 11:** Buddhist monk Quang Duc sets fire to himself in protest at Ngo Dinh Diem's government's treatment of Buddhists (South Vietnam's religious majority). Diem attacks Buddhist pagodas.
November 1: Diem is deposed and murdered in South Vietnam.
November 22: President Kennedy is **assassinated**. Lyndon Johnson becomes president.

1964	**January 30:** The South Vietnamese general Nguyen Khanh reclaims power in South Vietnam.
	August: In the Gulf of Tonkin, North Vietnamese boats attack US navy destroyers. The US government approves the Gulf of Tonkin Resolution to wage war against North Vietnam.
1965	**March 2:** Operation Rolling Thunder, a three-year US bombing campaign against North Vietnam, begins.
1968	**January 31:** The Tet Offensive begins—the North Vietnamese army captures key cities and towns in South Vietnam.
	March 16: The massacre of around 400 civilians at South Vietnamese village of My Lai takes place.
	May 10: Peace talks between the United States and North Vietnam begin—the start of a five-year process.
1969	**January 20:** Richard Nixon becomes President of the United States.
	September 2: Ho Chi Minh dies.
1971	**December:** The last Australian combat troops leave Vietnam.
1973	**January 15:** Nixon announces a ceasefire, which is followed by a peace agreement.
	March 29: The last US troops leave Vietnam.
1974	**August 9:** President Nixon resigns and is replaced by Gerald Ford.
1975	**April 30:** The North Vietnamese capture Saigon, the capital of South Vietnam.
1976	**July 2:** Vietnam becomes one county—the Socialist Republic of Vietnam. Saigon is renamed Ho Chi Minh City.

GLOSSARY

alliance an agreed joining of two or more people, countries, or organizations to work together for an agreed outcome

allies two or more people, countries, or organizations working together for an agreed outcome

ambushed attacked by surprise

amnesty an official pardon

ancestry the generations that have lived before a person

assassinated when an important person is deliberately killed

atrocities terrible acts often committed during war

bombardment a relentless attack

booby traps deadly devices hidden in harmless-looking places

Buddhist someone who practices Buddhism, the main religion in South Vietnam

ceasefire a command to stop attacks

civilians ordinary people who do not make up the military

colonial relating to when one country has control over another country

communist a person who believes in creating an equal society through government control of property and many other areas of life

corrupt dishonest, not good

crossfire gunfire from two or more directions

deserters soldiers who abandon the army

disillusioned no longer believing that something is what you once thought it was

evacuate to help to leave

fortified made stronger

herbicide chemical used to destroy plants or weeds

hostility hostile, or having aggressive feelings, toward someone or something

lethal deadly

massacre the brutal and widespread killing of several people

morale how uplifted or positive a person feels

morality rights and wrongs

neutral not allied to any side

opponents people who are acting against you

orphans children who have no parents because they have died

peasant an often-poor person who works on the land

persecuted hunted down

post-traumatic stress disorder (PTSD) a condition that can affect someone's mind after a terrible, traumatic experience

reconciliation becoming friends again after conflict

refugees people who must leave their home, and often their country, for their own safety

respite a break or relief from something difficult

tour of duty a length of time spent in a war zone

toxic poisonous

veterans men and women who have served in the armed forces

FIND OUT MORE

Books

DK. *The Vietnam War: The Definitive Illustrated History*.
Dorling Kindersley, 2021.

Longley, Kyle and Whitt, Jacqueline. *Grunts: The American Combat Soldier in Vietnam*. Routledge, 2020.

Rebman, Nick. *The Vietnam War* (Postwar America). North Star Editions, 2024.

Websites

Learn more about the Vietnam War at:
www.history.com/topics/vietnam-war/vietnam-war-history

Discover more about the conflict at:
www.historynet.com/vietnam-war

Learn more about the war at:
https://kids.britannica.com/kids/article/Vietnam-War/353899

Publisher's note to educators and parents:
All the websites featured above have been carefully reviewed to ensure that they are suitable for students. However, many websites change often, and we cannot guarantee that a site's future contents will continue to meet our high standards of educational value. Please be advised that students should be closely monitored whenever they access the Internet.

INDEX

About the Author

Kelly Roberts has written many history books for young people. In researching the eyewitness accounts in this book, she has learned more about the human experience of war and the devastation it caused for those who witnessed it.